MASTERING MONEY

WHAT YOUR PARENTS AND SCHOOLS NEVER TAUGHT YOU

JASON BROOME

Book Design by HmdPublishing

CONTENTS

INTRODUCTION

> *"The only way to get ahead financially is to spend less than you earn and invest the rest."*
> — **Dave Ramsey**

Imagine this: You're 24 years old, just landed your first full-time job, and finally have a steady paycheck. A few months in, you treat yourself to a weekend trip with friends, splurge on a new wardrobe, and maybe even pick up a few luxury gadgets. Before you know it, your credit card bill arrives, and it's a staggering amount. You scramble to make minimum payments, but the interest adds up. You wonder, "How did I get here?"

Now let's take it a step further, now you are 50 years old. You can see your retirement on the horizon. You dream of traveling and enjoying your golden years with the love of your life. Only one problem, you have been managing your finances like you did at 24 years old for your entire life. With no retirement, no savings, and no way to support yourself once you retire, the chances of traveling in your golden years aren't a reality. You're more likely to be working at a grocery store trying to make ends meet instead of traveling to Turks and Caicos and snorkeling with sea turtles.

This scenario is all too common. Young adults step into their lives with a lack of financial guidance leading to debt, stress, and living paycheck to paycheck. Two-thirds of Americans say they live this way—on the edge of financial instability. About 20% of Americans aged 50 and older have no retirement savings, according to recent surveys conducted by AARP and reported by sources like Kiplinger (Kiplinger.com) and Annuity.org(MediaRoom). This lack of savings is a significant concern as it points to potential financial insecurity for many as they approach retirement age. The surveys also highlight that a significant number of people in their 50s are worried about not having enough funds to sustain them during their retirement years. Yet, the key to avoiding these pitfalls is simple: financial literacy and budgeting.

My journey towards financial freedom wasn't easy. I was clueless about managing money. I used credit cards carelessly, never tracked my spending, and assumed the money would always be there. One day, checking out at the grocery store, the cashier politely leaned over and said your card was denied for insufficient funds. The financial freedom I thought I had was just an illusion. Not only was the illusion gone but because I continued using credit cards to fund everything I did, including starting a business, I was soon faced with filing bankruptcy to get out of my financial hell.

That wake-up call pushed me to learn about budgeting, saving, credit, and investing. It wasn't something I learned in school or from my parents, and most likely you haven't been taught this either—most young adults are financially unprepared. Financial literacy is one of the most important skills a young adult can acquire, yet it's rarely taught in school or by parents. Many young people enter adulthood without understanding basic principles like budgeting, saving, investing, and how to avoid debt traps. It's important to recognize that managing your money isn't just about making a lot of it—it's about understanding how to make smart decisions with the money you do have.

I do want to be clear that although I have a bachelor's degree in Public Administration and a master's degree in Accountancy, I'm no finance guru. This eBook was created based on my journey, the lessons I have learned, and the things I would have done differently had I known. It is the guide I wish I had when I started my financial journey.

The practical, actionable financial advice in this book, if put into practice, will set you on the path to long-term financial success. Each chapter will cover a financial topic that will help you manage your money better. Through personal stories, real-life examples, and straightforward advice, I will walk you through how to create a budget, understand your spending habits, and plan for the future. Whether you're a college student learning how to stretch your income, a young professional navigating debt, or in mid-life ready to get a handle on your finances, this guide will empower you to take control of your finances.

The key to your success is action and going through the accompanying exercises. These exercises will walk you through steps designed to help you put what is being learned into action.

FINANCIAL
LITERACY

CHAPTER

01

THE IMPORTANCE OF FINANCIAL LITERACY

"An investment in knowledge pays the best interest."
— Benjamin Franklin.

The importance of financial literacy cannot be overstated. When I think about the learning curve of my own life because of a lack of financial literacy, it is unbelievable. As you have read regarding my journey, from my very first credit card experience to trying to get an auto loan, to my debt, and ultimately filing bankruptcy, any amount of financial literacy could have prevented a lot of upheaval in my life. What do we mean by "financial literacy"?

Financial literacy is the ability to understand and effectively use various financial skills, including personal financial management, budgeting, and investing. It is crucial for navigating life's financial challenges and opportunities and helps one make informed decisions about their finances. This chapter explores the importance of financial literacy, real-world examples of its impact, techniques to improve financial literacy, tools that aid in this education, and exercises to enhance learning and application.

Significance of Financial Literacy

Financial literacy empowers individuals by equipping them with the knowledge to make informed financial decisions, which is vital for achieving personal financial success and stability. The benefits include:

1. **Better Money Management**: Understanding the basics of budgeting and money management helps individuals control their spending, save for future goals, and prepare for emergencies.

2. **Debt Management**: Knowledge of how credit works and the implications of accumulating debt allows individuals to make smarter decisions about borrowing, including how to manage loans and credit cards effectively.

3. **Investment Acumen**: Financial literacy enhances one's understanding of investment products, the risks involved, and the potential returns. This allows for better evaluation of in-

vestment opportunities, leading to more sound investment choices.

4. **Protection Against Fraud**: An informed individual is less likely to fall victim to fraud as they are more aware of common scams and understand how to protect their finances.

Techniques to Achieve Financial Literacy

1. **Educational Workshops and Seminars**: Attend workshops, seminars, and webinars on personal finance topics. These sessions are often held by financial institutions, community centers, or online platforms.

2. **Reading Books and Articles**: Read widely on financial topics. Books like "Rich Dad, Poor Dad" by Robert Kiyosaki and "The Total Money Makeover" by Dave Ramsey provide foundational knowledge and strategies for personal finance.

3. **Online Courses**: Enroll in online courses on platforms like Coursera, Udemy, or Khan Academy, which offer lessons on everything from basic budgeting to advanced investment strategies.

4. **Consulting with Financial Advisors**: Regular consultations with financial experts can provide personalized advice tailored to your financial situation and goals.

Tools to Help Achieve Financial Literacy

1. **Personal Finance Apps**: Apps like Mint, YNAB (You Need A Budget), and Personal Capital help track spending and budget and monitor investments, providing practical, hands-on experience with managing personal finances.

2. **Financial Planning Software**: Tools like Quicken or Microsoft Money provide comprehensive platforms for managing your finances and can teach users about budgeting,

forecasting, and more through direct interaction with their finances.

3. **Investment Simulators**: Platforms like Investopedia's stock simulator offer risk-free environments to practice trading stocks, which helps users learn the mechanics of the stock market without financial risk.

Financial literacy is not merely an academic requirement but a practical necessity that empowers individuals to navigate the complexities of the financial world with confidence and success. Achieving financial literacy is an ongoing process that adapts to changes in your personal circumstances and the broader economic environment. By actively engaging, you can enhance your understanding and confidence in handling financial matters.

I hope you have increased your financial literacy and have started your first budget or improved on an existing one. I do not doubt if you put this information to use and go through the exercises you will be able to avoid many of the mistakes I made as a young adult. The key is to put the information into practice and use it. Do not end up working your entire life just to make ends meet. Save, invest, and have the life you have always dreamed of, whatever that may be. It's right there staring at you; you just have to grab it. The power is in you!

CHAPTER

02

THE IMPORTANCE OF BUDGETING

"The best way to stick to your budget is to start it before you spend."

— John Di Lemme.

As a young adult, my budget consisted of getting an insufficient funds notice for a check I wrote in the mail -you heard that correctly, a check was handwritten, and I didn't know there was a problem until I got a notice in the mail- or have a utility shut off because a check bounced. The bounced check and utility being shut off were just the beginning of the problems. I also had to deal with insufficient funds fees, fees from the utility company for the returned check, the late payment fee, and the fee for the utility reconnection. I treated my finances like I had an endless supply of money, which I didn't. All of this could have been avoided with the most basic of budgets to ensure the funds were in my account before I did any spending to avoid all this chaos, saving me time and money.

What is Budgeting

Budgeting simply is the process of creating a spending plan for your money. This spending plan allows you to determine in advance whether you will have enough money to do the things you need to do or would like to do. It isn't just about restricting spending but about understanding your financial situation so you can make informed financial decisions.

A typical budget includes:

- **Income:** All sources of incoming money, such as wages, salaries, bonuses, interest, dividends, and other revenue.
- **Fixed Expenses:** Regular, unchanging costs, such as rent, mortgage payments, insurance premiums, and utilities.
- **Variable Expenses:** Costs that fluctuate monthly, like groceries, entertainment, clothing, and gas.
- **Savings and Investments:** Money set aside for emergencies, future purchases, investments, or retirement.
- **Debt Repayments:** Any payments toward loans, credit cards, or other debt obligations.

Why Budget?

The primary reason to create a budget is to help you keep your finances under control by keeping track of how much money you're spending and where it's going. It is a fundamental tool in managing your finances. It is essential for achieving financial goals, whether that involves saving for a down payment on a house, setting aside money for a vacation, or simply ensuring you never run out of money each month.

Budgeting plays a crucial role in fostering a deeper understanding of key financial concepts, including:

1. **Achieving Financial Goals:** A budget provides a clear framework for setting and achieving financial goals, like saving for a vacation, buying a house, or retiring comfortably. By outlining income and expenses, budgeting helps allocate funds toward goals and track progress.
2. **Spending Control:** With a budget, you have a defined limit on spending. This can prevent impulsive purchases and help avoid the stress of financial shortfalls.
3. **Debt Management:** By setting aside funds specifically for debt repayment, a budget enables people to pay down debt systematically, reducing interest payments over time.
4. **Improving Financial Habits:** Creating and sticking to a budget promotes disciplined spending and saving habits, fostering a better relationship with money.
5. **Reducing Financial Stress:** With a budget, there's a clear plan for covering bills and saving for the future, helping to reduce the stress associated with financial uncertainty and surprises.
6. **Emergency Preparedness:** By incorporating an emergency fund into the budget, people can build a financial cushion to rely on during unexpected events, such as job loss, medical expenses, or home repairs.

Budgeting Techniques

Today, various budgeting techniques are available, many of which leverage automation to simplify the process. Here are a few of the most basic budgeting techniques that can be done with a pen and paper or a simple spreadsheet. At the end of the chapter, you will be able to put your knowledge to work using the given exercises.

Budget Systems

1. **Envelope System** This is a cash-based budgeting system where you divide your cash into envelopes for different spending categories like groceries, entertainment, and transportation. Once the cash in an envelope is gone, you can't spend any more in that category until the next budget period begins. This method is excellent for those who have a hard time sticking to their budget.

2. **Zero-Based Budget** Every dollar you earn is assigned a job, whether it's going towards bills, savings, or investments, ensuring there are zero dollars left unassigned. This technique can be very effective for achieving aggressive financial goals.

3. **50/30/20 Rule** This rule suggests that 50% of your income should go towards necessities, 30% towards wants, and 20% towards savings and debt repayment. It's a simpler approach and good for those new to budgeting.

4. **The 60% Solution** A variation of the 50/30/20, this method suggests that 60% of your gross income should go towards committed expenses (including savings), and the remaining 40% is split among retirement contributions, short-term savings, and fun money.

Budget Tool Resources

1. **Mint**: This app allows users to create budgets and track their spending. It automatically categorizes transactions

from linked credit and debit cards and tracks them against a budget.

2. **You Need A Budget (YNAB)**: This app is based on the zero-based budgeting system and provides users with tools to improve their spending habits and gain control over their finances.

3. **EveryDollar**: Developed by personal finance guru Dave Ramsey, this tool focuses on zero-based budgeting and offers both free and premium versions.

You should have a budget for no reason other than to avoid the chaos from my example. I lived paycheck to paycheck in those days and needed to know where all the money was going. Even if you aren't living paycheck to paycheck, budgeting is still important. Not merely as an exercise in financial limitation but as an essential tool for economic freedom. It provides detailed insights into one's financial habits, empowering individuals to make informed financial decisions, prioritize expenses, and ultimately achieve financial stability. Whether you are a student, a single professional, or managing a household, budgeting can pave the way to financial success and security. As we continue through the rest of the book, you will see that everything leads back to budgeting. Budgeting is the key. Get this right, and you will be successful. The only way to learn is to do it, so take some time before going to the next chapter, go through the budgeting exercises, and create a budget.

Monthly Budgeting Worksheet

Here is a simple and effective monthly budget. By documenting all income sources and expenses, you can get a clear picture of your financial health and make necessary adjustments. This can be easily created in Excel or Google Sheets and be creative to your specific situation and needs adding columns, rows, and change titles.

Worksheet Format:

Income Sources	**Amount ($)**
Job Salary	
Side Hustles	
Other Income	
Total Income	
Fixed Expenses	
Rent/Mortgage	
Utilities	
Insurance	
Debt Repayment	
Total Fixed Expenses	
Variable Expenses	
Groceries	
Transportation	
Entertainment	
Dining Out	
Misc. Spending	
Total Variable Expenses	
Savings	
Emergency Fund	
Retirement Savings	
Other Savings Goals	
Total Savings	
Remaining Balance (Total Income - Total Expenses and Savings)	

Instructions for Use:

1. **Income Sources**: Document all sources of income you expect to receive during the month, including your primary job, any side hustles, and other sources like investments or rental income.

2. **Fixed Expenses**: List all fixed expenses that are the same each month, such as rent or mortgage payments, utility bills, and insurance premiums.

3. **Variable Expenses**: Enter estimates for variable expenses that can change monthly, like groceries, transportation costs, and entertainment.

4. **Savings**: Allocate amounts you plan to save during the month across various categories, including emergency funds, retirement accounts, and other specific saving goals.

5. **Calculations**:

   - Calculate **Total Income** by adding up all income sources.
   - Sum up all fixed and variable expenses.
   - Deduct the total expenses and savings from your total income to find the **Remaining Balance**.

6. **Adjustments**: Review the Remaining Balance. If the number is negative, look for areas in variable expenses where spending can be reduced. If the balance is positive, consider increasing your savings contributions.

Outcome:

- This exercise will provide you with a hands-on approach to creating a budget that fits within your means. Regularly using this worksheet can help you better understand your financial flow and improve your ability to manage money effectively.

Implementation Tips

- **Regular Review**: Update and review this worksheet monthly to track changes in your financial situation and adjust your budget accordingly.

- **Digital Adaptation**: Consider using a digital spreadsheet to maintain this worksheet for easier calculations and updates.
- **Continuous Improvement**: As you become more familiar with your spending habits, refine your categories and budgeting strategy to better suit your financial goals.

1. **Envelope System Worksheet**

This worksheet helps implement the envelope system, where cash is allocated to different categories, and spending is limited to the amount available in each envelope.

Worksheet Format:

Envelope Category	Budget Amount	Expenses	Remaining Balance
Groceries			
Entertainment			
Transportation			
Utilities			
Misc.			
Total			

Instructions for Use:

- **Envelope Category**: Label envelopes with categories like Groceries, Entertainment, etc.
- **Budget Amount**: Fill each envelope with the cash amount budgeted for that category for the month.
- **Expenses**: Record each expense you pay out of the envelope.
- **Remaining Balance**: Update this as you spend, showing what's left.

Outcome:

- Control spending by physically limiting available cash, making it easier to adhere to budget limits.

2. **Zero-Based Budget Worksheet**

This worksheet is designed to help you allocate every dollar of income, ensuring nothing is left unassigned.

Worksheet Format:

Category	Planned Amount	Actual Spending	Difference
Income			
Rent/Mortgage			
Utilities			
Groceries			
Savings			
Debt Repayment			
Miscellaneous			
Total Expenses			

Instructions for Use:

- **Category**: List all income sources and expense categories.
- **Planned Amount/Actual Spending**: Start with your total income at the top and subtract expenses as you list them.
- **Difference**: Regularly compare planned spending against actual to adjust where necessary.

Outcome:

- Ensures all income is purposefully spent or saved, leaving zero dollars unassigned.

3. **50/30/20 Rule Budget Worksheet**

This budget is divided into three simple categories: necessities, wants, and savings/debt repayment.

Worksheet Format:

Category	Percentage	Amount	Actual Spending	Difference
Necessities	**50%**			
Wants	**30%**			
Savings/Debt	**20%**			
Total	**100%**			

Instructions for Use:

- **Percentage**: Allocate 50% of your income to necessities, 30% to wants, and 20% to savings and debt repayment.
- **Amount**: Calculate the dollar amounts for each category based on your total income.
- **Actual Spending and Difference**: Monitor your actual spending versus the budgeted amounts.

Outcome:

- Simplifies budget management and helps balance essential needs, personal desires, and financial growth.

4. **The 60% Solution Worksheet**

This variation of the 50/30/20 rule focuses more income on committed expenses and savings.

Worksheet Format:

Category	Percentage	Amount	Actual Spending	Difference
Committed Expenses	**60%**			

Retirement Savings	**10%**			
Short-term Savings	**10%**			
Fun Money	**20%**			
Total	**100%**			

Instructions for Use:

- **Percentage**: Assign 60% of your income to essential and committed expenses, 20% to fun or discretionary spending, and 20% to savings (split into retirement and short-term goals).
- **Amount**: Convert these percentages into actual dollar amounts based on your income.
- **Actual Spending and Difference**: Keep track of spending in each category to ensure alignment with the budgeted percentages.

Outcome:

- Provides a structured but flexible framework that emphasizes saving while allowing for personal spending.

Implementation Tips

- **Regular Updates**: Review and update these worksheets regularly to ensure they accurately reflect your financial activities and adjustments.
- **Digital Tracking**: Consider using digital tools or apps that can automate some of these calculations and provide real-time insights into your budgeting performance.
- **Personal Adjustment**: Feel free to adjust the categories and percentages to better fit your unique financial situation and goals.

CHAPTER

03

LIVING WITHIN YOUR MEANS

> *"Too many people spend money they haven't earned, to buy things they don't want, to impress people they don't like."*
> **— Will Rogers.**

The concept of living within your means is probably the most difficult to accept. For me, I don't like the idea that there are some things I just cannot afford. We all want to take that trip to the beach or buy a new vehicle instead of a used one. But we also have to be able to pay our bills and have money for our future retirement. Living within your means doesn't mean you can never have a new car or take a trip to the beach, but, as we have discussed, you may have to set a financial goal to get there.

Living within your means involves spending less money than you earn and is crucial for long-term financial health and stability. It prevents debt accumulation, enables savings for future needs, and prepares for unexpected financial crises. This detailed explanation will cover the importance of this financial principle, provide real-world examples, discuss techniques and tools to help maintain this lifestyle, and suggest exercises to reinforce good spending habits.

The Importance of Living Within Your Means

Not living within your means often results in mounting debt, financial stress, and the inability to save for future goals like retirement or emergencies. Adopting a lifestyle within your means lays the foundation for financial security and supports the achievement of long-term goals. This practice is essential for several reasons:

- **Prevents Debt**: Overspending often leads to debt. By living within your means, you avoid relying on credit to cover daily expenses, thus avoiding costly interest payments and potential debt spirals.
- **Builds Savings**: It frees up income that can be diverted towards savings and investments, helping to build a financial cushion and fund future goals like retirement or home ownership.

- **Reduces Stress**: Financial overextension is a common source of stress. Knowing that you are spending within your budget can alleviate anxiety related to finances.
- **Ensures Sustainability**: Long-term financial health requires sustainable spending habits that don't rely on uncertain future income increases.

Real-World Examples

1. **Sarah's Budget Adjustment**: When Sarah received a promotion with a salary increase, instead of upgrading her lifestyle, she chose to maintain her previous standard of living. She used the extra income to repay her student loans faster and increased her retirement savings contributions.
2. **Mike's Car Purchase**: Mike needed to replace his car. Despite qualifying for a more expensive model, he chose a modest car that was reliable but not luxurious, ensuring his car payments did not exceed 10% of his monthly income, thus maintaining his financial comfort zone.

Techniques to Live Within Your Means

1. **Budget Creation**: The cornerstone of living within your means is a realistic budget that tracks all income and expenses. It should include savings as a necessary "expense" to ensure it is prioritized.
2. **Needs vs. Wants Analysis**: Distinguish between necessities (needs) and desires (wants). Prioritize spending on essentials and allow discretionary spending only if your budget permits.
3. **Use Cash Instead of Credit**: Using cash for daily transactions can help you visualize and control spending more effectively than using credit cards.
4. **Avoid Lifestyle Inflation**: As your income increases, resist the temptation to increase your spending proportionally.

Maintain your standard of living and direct extra income toward savings or debt repayment.

5. **Save Before You Spend:** Commit to saving a portion of your income for emergencies or investments before addressing discretionary spending.
6. **Regular Financial Reviews**: Periodically review your financial situation and adjust your budget as needed. This helps catch and correct any drift towards overspending.

Tools to Help You Live Within Your Means

1. **Mint**: This budgeting app provides an excellent overview of your financial situation, helping you track spending, create budgets, and set financial goals.
2. **You Need A Budget (YNAB)**: YNAB teaches users to treat every dollar with intention, which is fundamental to living within your means. It also encourages changing spending behavior based on available funds.
3. **Envelope Budgeting System**: A traditional method where cash for various budget categories is kept in separate envelopes. Once the cash in an envelope is gone, no more spending is allowed in that category until the next budget period.

Living within your means is not about deprivation but about making informed and conscious choices with your money. It is a sustainable practice that builds a strong financial foundation, enabling you to achieve your long-term goals while avoiding the pitfalls of debt and financial instability. For example, your credit score. We have discussed the importance of credit score and how it can impact your buying power, but as you can see, it also affects what living within your means can look like. Higher score + lower interest rate = buying power. This directly impacts what living within your means looks like.

By implementing these techniques, using the suggested tools, and regularly engaging in the exercises, you can enhance your ability to manage your finances effectively and ensure your spending habits support a stable and secure financial future.

CHAPTER

04

UNDERSTANDING MINDFUL SPENDING

We have all made purchases without considering how they will impact us financially or if they support our goals. Probably because we didn't have any financial goals or a budget set to begin with, I lived that way for many years. A perfect example is Christmas time. Every year, I would spend the year paying off credit card debt, and just when I thought I was making progress, it would be Christmas time again, and I was buying gifts with credit cards. I'm thinking about the pressure of gift-giving and getting caught up in the mindless spending of the holidays instead of looking at my goals and budget.

Mindful spending is an approach to personal finance that involves being conscious and intentional with how you use your money. It's about aligning your spending habits with your values, goals, and financial circumstances to promote greater financial well-being and life satisfaction. Here's a detailed explanation of what mindful spending involves and how to practice it:

Key Principles of Mindful Spending

1. **Awareness**: Being fully aware of where your money is going and whether those expenditures contribute to your long-term happiness and goals.

2. **Intentionality**: Every spending decision is made deliberately, not impulsively or habitually, ensuring that it serves a real purpose in your life.

3. **Alignment with Values**: Spending money on things that truly matter to you, reflect your values, and enhance your life, rather than on items that don't bring lasting satisfaction.

4. **Financial Control**: Maintaining control over your finances by avoiding debt, managing your budget, and ensuring that your spending does not exceed your income.

How to Practice Mindful Spending

1. **Track Your Expenses**: Start by tracking where every dollar goes. This can be eye-opening and help you identify areas where your spending does not align with your priorities.
2. **Set Financial Goals**: Define what you want to achieve with your money. Goals could be as immediate as saving for a vacation or as long-term as achieving financial independence.
3. **Create a Budget**: Use a budget to plan your spending in a way that helps you reach your goals while covering all necessities. Stick to your budget to maintain discipline in your spending habits.
4. **Question Each Purchase**: Before making a purchase, ask yourself a few questions: Do I need this? How often will I use it? Does it add value to my life? Can I afford it without using credit?
5. **Prioritize Experiences Over Things**: Research shows that experiences bring more lasting happiness than material goods. Consider spending more on experiences like travel, learning new skills, or quality time with loved ones, as they often provide greater lasting fulfillment than material items.
6. **Cultivate Gratitude**: Being grateful for what you already have can reduce the desire for new purchases. Regular reflection on your blessings can encourage more contentment with less consumption.
7. **Use Technology Wisely**: Leverage apps and tools that track your spending and help you stick to your budget. These can automate some aspects of financial management, making it easier to stay mindful.
8. **Regular Financial Reviews**: Periodically review your financial situation and adjust your spending as necessary. Life changes, and so might your values and financial goals.

Mindful spending isn't about restricting yourself—it's about making more fulfilling choices with your financial resources. By spending mindfully, you can enhance not just your well-being but also contribute positively to broader societal and environmental goals by choosing to support sustainable and ethical products and services.

Techniques for Mindful Spending

1. **Budget for Values**: Create a budget that reflects your values by categorizing spending into "needs," "wants," and "values." Allocate funds in a way that prioritizes expenses that match your personal and ethical values.

2. **Needs vs. Wants Analysis**: Regularly assess your purchases by asking whether they are needs (essential for basic living) or wants (things that enhance or improve your life). Further analyze wants by determining how much joy or value they add to your life.

3. **The 30-Day Rule**: For non-essential purchases, particularly expensive ones, implement a 30-day waiting period. If you still feel the purchase is necessary after this time, it's likely a valid expense.

4. **Mindful Review of Recurring Expenses**: Regularly review subscriptions and recurring charges. Cancel any that you no longer use or that don't align with your values or long-term goals.

Mindful Spending Tool Resources

1. **Mint**: This budgeting app categorizes your spending and helps you see where your money goes each month, making it easier to adjust habits that aren't in line with your values.

2. **You Need A Budget (YNAB)**: YNAB emphasizes giving every dollar a job and encourages you to allocate funds according to your values and goals.

3. **PocketGuard**: This app shows how much disposable income you have after accounting for bills, goals, and essentials, helping you avoid overspending.

Mindful spending isn't just about saving money—it's about spending smart and living in a way that brings genuine fulfillment and aligns with your personal goals. By incorporating the described techniques, tools, and exercises into your daily life, you can enhance your financial well-being and live a richer, more intentional life. If you haven't figured it out yet, the key to all of this is budgeting. You must establish a budget and be disciplined enough to stick to it.

Mindful Spending Worksheets

Worksheet 1: Value Alignment Check

Objective: To evaluate how well your spending aligns with your declared values.

Worksheet Format:

Value	Expense Category	Amount Spent	Percentage of Total Spend	Aligned (Yes/No)	Notes
Health	Gym Membership	$50	5%	Yes	Essential for well-being
Education	Books	$100	10%	Yes	Invest in personal development
Entertainment	Movie Tickets	$60	6%	No	Reduce to save for more important goals
[Add More Rows as Needed]					

Instructions for Use:

1. **List Top Five Values**: Write down your top five personal values.
2. **Categorize Last Month's Expenses**: Assign each expense to a value.
3. **Evaluate**: Assess whether each spending category truly supports the corresponding value. Calculate what percentage of your total spending each category represents.
4. **Adjust**: Determine which expenses need to be adjusted to better align with your values.

Outcome:

- Gain insight into how your spending reflects your values and identify areas for adjustment to enhance overall life satisfaction.

Worksheet 2: Needs vs. Wants Table

Objective: Differentiate between essential and non-essential expenditures.

Worksheet Format:

Date	Item	Cost	Category (Need/ Want)	Value Added	Action (Keep/ Reduce/Eliminate)
10/01	Coffee at Cafe	$5	Want	Low	Reduce
10/02	Groceries	$150	Need	High	Keep
[Add More Rows as Needed]					

Instructions for Use:

1. **Record Every Purchase**: Log every expenditure for the month, detailing what you bought, how much it cost, and whether it was a need or a want.
2. **Value Added**: Assess how much value or joy each purchase added to your life.
3. **Decide Action**: Decide whether to keep, reduce, or eliminate each 'want' based on its value added.

Outcome:

- Develop a clearer understanding of your spending patterns and make conscious decisions to focus more on needs and meaningful wants.

Worksheet 3: 30-Day Purchase Plan

Objective: Implement a waiting period to evaluate the necessity of non-essential purchases.

Worksheet Format:

Item	Cost	Date Considered	Date Reviewed	Still Needed (Yes/No)	Decision (Proceed/ Cancel)
New Smartphone	$999	10/01	10/31	No	Cancel
[Add More Rows as Needed]					

Instructions for Use:

1. **List Desired Purchases**: Whenever you consider making a non-essential purchase, list the item and its cost.
2. **Mark the Date**: Note the date when you first thought of buying the item.

3. **Review After 30 Days**: After 30 days, review each item and decide if it is still necessary or desirable.

4. **Make a Decision**: Decide whether to proceed with the purchase or cancel it based on the review.

Outcome:

- Reduce impulse purchases by introducing a deliberate decision-making process, ensuring your purchases are thoughtful and genuinely needed.

Implementation Tips

- **Regular Review**: Update and review these worksheets regularly to keep track of spending changes and evaluate the effectiveness of your mindful spending practices.
- **Digital Adaptation**: For ease of use and modification, consider maintaining these worksheets in a digital format.
- **Reflect and Adjust**: Use these exercises not just for tracking but as a foundation for regular financial reflection and adjustment to enhance your financial well-being.

Worksheet 1: 30-Day Impulse Spending Freeze

This worksheet helps you track non-essential spending impulses and evaluate them over a 30-day period.

Worksheet Format:

Date	Item Considered	Cost	Still Want It? (Yes/No)	Decision (Buy/ Not Buy)
10/01	Trendy Coffee Mug	$15		
10/02	Hardcover Novel	$20		
[Add more rows as needed]				

Instructions for Use:

1. **Item Considered**: Each time you consider buying a non-essential item, record the item and its cost.
2. **Still Want It?**: After 30 days, revisit this column to note if you still desire the item.
3. **Decision**: Decide if you will buy the item or not based on your reflection after the waiting period.

Outcome:

- Distinguish between impulse purchases and actual needs, helping reinforce spending discipline.

Worksheet 2: Zero-Based Budgeting Challenge

This worksheet helps you allocate every dollar you earn to expenses, savings, or debt repayment, ensuring your income equals your expenditures.

Worksheet Format:

Category	Budgeted Amount	Actual Spending	Difference
Rent	$800	$800	$0
Groceries	$300	$285	$15
Dining Out	$100	$150	-$50
Savings	$200	$200	$0
[Add more rows as needed]			

Instructions for Use:

1. **Category**: List all categories of your expenses, including savings and debt repayments.
2. **Budgeted Amount**: Assign a planned amount to each category, ensuring total spending matches total income.

3. **Actual Spending**: At the end of the month, fill in what you actually spent.
4. **Difference**: Calculate the difference between budgeted and actual spending.

Outcome:

- Ensure every dollar is accounted for, promoting disciplined financial management and preventing overspending.

Worksheet 3: Weekly Money Date

This worksheet is for scheduling regular weekly reviews of your financial status, allowing you to adjust as needed to stay on budget.

Worksheet Format:

Week Ending	Income	Total Spent	Over/Under Budget	Adjustments Needed
10/07	$1,200	$1,150	$50 Under	None
10/14	$1,200	$1,300	$100 Over	Cut dining out
[Add more rows as needed]				

Instructions for Use:

1. **Week Ending**: Mark the end of each week.
2. **Income**: Record the total income received that week.
3. **Total Spent**: Sum up all expenses for the week.
4. **Over/Under Budget**: Calculate whether you are over or under your weekly budget.
5. **Adjustments Needed**: Note any adjustments you need to make for the following week.

Outcome:

- Maintain a regular check on your financial health, ensuring that your spending habits align with your financial goals and living within your means.

SAVINGS

CHAPTER

05

THE NECESSITY OF AN EMERGENCY FUND

"The best time to repair the roof is when the sun is shining."
— John F. Kennedy.

An emergency fund is an essential part of financial planning that provides a safety net of cash to cover unexpected expenses or financial emergencies without the need to incur debt. These funds are crucial for maintaining financial stability during times of uncertainty, such as sudden medical emergencies, urgent car repairs, or unforeseen job loss.

For most of my life, I didn't have an emergency fund. When I didn't have the money to pay a bill, I would use a credit card, putting myself in debt and paying interest on the debt. It was a chaotic cycle of trying to survive. Even though I didn't make much money, it was still avoidable. With the use of -you guessed it- a budget, I could have established an emergency fund. But I didn't know then what I know now. Even before you start saving for retirement or that vacation, you need to first establish an emergency fund that you do not touch for any reason other than an emergency. Once you have that safety net, then look to retirement or that vacation.

Importance of an Emergency Fund

1. **Prevents Debt**: An emergency fund can prevent you from falling into debt when unexpected expenses arise. Without it, you may be forced to take on high-interest credit card debt or personal loans.

2. **Reduces Stress**: Knowing you have a financial cushion can reduce stress and provide peace of mind during times of hardship.

3. **Improves Financial Security**: An emergency fund is a key component of a solid financial foundation, offering the security to navigate through life's unexpected challenges without jeopardizing your financial future.

4. **Job Loss**: Tom, a marketing executive, suddenly lost his job due to company downsizing. Fortunately, he had built an emergency fund equal to six months of living expenses, giving him the financial breathing room to focus on finding

a new job without the immediate pressure to compromise on his next position.

5. **Medical Emergency**: Sara experienced a sudden medical emergency requiring hospitalization. Her emergency fund covered the high deductible on her insurance plan, which allowed her to receive the necessary treatment without financial strain.

6. **Home Repairs**: The Jackson family's basement flooded unexpectedly. Thanks to their emergency fund, they could pay for the repair services and necessary renovations without going into debt.

Techniques to Create an Emergency Fund

1. **Determine the Size of the Fund**: Most financial advisors recommend saving between three to six months' worth of living expenses. Evaluate your job security, health, and potential major expenses to decide the right size for your fund.

2. **Start Small**: If saving several months' worth of expenses seems daunting, start small. Aim to initially save $500 or $1,000, then gradually increase your savings goal as your financial situation improves.

3. **Set Up Automatic Transfers**: Automate your savings by setting up automatic transfers from your checking account to a savings account dedicated to your emergency fund. This ensures regular contributions and reduces the temptation to spend the money elsewhere.

4. **Cut Unnecessary Expenses**: Review your budget for areas where you can cut back, such as dining out, subscriptions, or luxury items. Redirect these savings into your emergency fund.

5. **Increase Income**: Consider increasing your income through side hustles, overtime work, or selling unwanted items. Apply all additional income directly to your emergency fund until it reaches your target size.

Tools to Help You Create an Emergency Fund

1. **High-Yield Savings Account**: Use a high-yield savings account to separate your emergency fund from your regular checking account. These accounts offer higher interest rates, helping your savings grow faster.

2. **Budgeting Apps**: Tools like Mint, YNAB (You Need A Budget), and EveryDollar can help you track your expenses and manage your budget more effectively. Use them to identify savings opportunities for your emergency fund.

3. **Automatic Savings Apps**: Apps like Acorns or Digit analyze your spending habits and automatically transfer small amounts to savings, which can be designated for your emergency fund.

An emergency fund is not just a financial buffer but a fundamental component of a sound financial plan, ensuring you can handle life's surprises without compromising your financial stability. By implementing these techniques, using the suggested tools, and engaging in the exercises, you can build and maintain an adequate emergency fund to protect yourself and your loved ones from unforeseen financial shocks.

Emergency Fund Worksheets

Worksheet 1: Emergency Fund Planning Worksheet

Objective: To plan and track the establishment of your emergency fund.

Worksheet Format:

Month	Monthly Income	Monthly Savings Goal	Actual Amount Saved	Cumulative Savings
January				
February				
March				
[Add more rows as needed]				

Instructions for Use:

1. **Monthly Income**: Enter your total expected income for each month.
2. **Monthly Savings Goal**: Set a target amount you aim to save each month toward your emergency fund.
3. **Actual Amount Saved**: At the end of the month, record the actual amount you were able to save.
4. **Cumulative Savings**: Calculate the total amount saved towards the emergency fund up to that month.

Outcome:

- Visualize and track your progress toward achieving a fully funded emergency fund.

Worksheet 2: Expense Reduction Challenge

Objective: Identify and reduce unnecessary spending to increase emergency fund savings.

Worksheet Format:

Category	Last Month's Spending	Target Reduction (%)	Amount Saved	Redirected to Emergency Fund
Dining Out		50		
Entertainment		50		
Subscriptions		50		
[Add more rows as need-ed]				

Instructions for Use:

1. **Last Month's Spending**: Fill in how much you spent last month in each non-essential category.
2. **Target Reduction (%)**: Set a percentage by how much you aim to reduce spending in these categories.
3. **Amount Saved**: At the end of the month, calculate how much you saved due to spending reductions.
4. **Redirected to Emergency Fund**: Indicate how much of the saved money you transferred to your emergency fund.

Outcome:

- Efficiently redirect saved funds to boost your emergency savings, fostering better spending habits.

Worksheet 3: Income Augmentation Plan

Objective: Develop and track strategies to increase income specifically for boosting emergency fund contributions.

Worksheet Format:

Side Hustle/ Freelance Job	Expected Income	Actual Income Earned	Contributed to Emergency Fund
Tutoring			
Freelance Writing			
Etsy Shop			
[Add more rows as needed]			

Instructions for Use:

1. **Side Hustle/Freelance Job**: List potential or current side jobs or freelance work.
2. **Expected Income**: Estimate how much you expect to earn from each activity.
3. **Actual Income Earned**: Record the actual income received at the end of the period.
4. **Contributed to Emergency Fund**: Document how much of this income was added to your emergency fund.

Outcome:

- Utilize additional income streams to enhance your emergency fund savings, accelerating your financial security efforts.

Implementation Tips

- **Regular Updates**: Regularly update these worksheets to reflect actual income, spending, and savings. This helps in maintaining accuracy and making necessary adjustments.
- **Digital Tracking**: Use spreadsheet functionalities such as sum formulas and conditional formatting to automate calculations and highlight important data.

- **Review and Adjust**: Periodically review your progress and strategies. If you find certain methods are not as effective, consider adjusting your approach or trying new strategies to meet your goals.

These worksheets provide a structured approach to managing your finances with the specific aim of building a robust emergency fund. They encourage discipline, strategic planning, and regular review of financial practices.

Worksheet 1: Income Stream Brainstorming Session

Objective: Identify potential new income streams based on your skills, hobbies, and resources.

Worksheet Format:

Skills/Hobbies	Possible Income Streams	Estimated Earning Potential	Initial Steps to Monetize
Photography	Selling photos online	$200 per month	Create an account on stock photo websites
Baking	Home-based bakery	$500 per month	Research local food regulations, create a menu
[Add more rows as needed]			

Instructions for Use:

1. **Skills/Hobbies**: List all your current skills and hobbies.

2. **Possible Income Streams**: Brainstorm ways to monetize each skill or hobby.

3. **Estimated Earning Potential**: Research or estimate how much you could potentially earn from each stream.

4. **Initial Steps to Monetize**: List the first few steps needed to start monetizing each skill or hobby.

Outcome:

- A comprehensive list of viable income streams tailored to your unique skills and interests.

Worksheet 2: Financial Independence Roadmap

Objective: Develop a detailed plan for achieving financial independence by listing and planning income streams.

Worksheet Structure:

Income Stream	Current Income	Potential Income	Action Steps	Timeline
Freelance Writing	$1,000/ month	$2,000/ month	Increase client base	Next 6 months
Real Estate Rentals	$1,500/ month	$2,500/ month	Acquire another property	Next 2 years
[Add more rows as needed]				

Instructions for Use:

1. **Income Stream**: Identify all current and potential income streams.
2. **Current Income**: Document how much you currently earn from each stream.
3. **Potential Income**: Estimate how much you could potentially earn if expanded.
4. **Action Steps**: List concrete steps to increase earnings from each income stream.
5. **Timeline**: Set realistic timelines for accomplishing each action step.

Outcome:

- A strategic plan with clear steps and timelines aimed at increasing your income and moving towards financial independence.

Worksheet 3: Investment Analysis Exercise

Objective: Evaluate and optimize your investment strategies to maximize returns and minimize risks.

Worksheet Structure:

Investment Type	Potential Return	Risks	Current Investment	Planned Investment
Stocks	7% average return	Market volatility	$10,000	$15,000
Bonds	3% average return	Low risk	$5,000	$5,000
Real Estate	6% average return	High initial cost	$20,000	$30,000
[Add more rows as needed]				

Instructions for Use:

1. **Investment Type**: List various types of investments you are interested in or currently have.
2. **Potential Return**: Research and list the average or expected returns for each investment type.
3. **Risks**: Identify and list the risks associated with each type of investment.
4. **Current Investment**: Note how much you currently have invested in each type.
5. **Planned Investment**: Plan how much you aim to invest going forward, considering your financial goals and risk tolerance.

Outcome:

- A diversified investment portfolio that balances risk and maximizes potential returns based on thorough analysis and strategic planning.

HOW
MUCH
DO
YOU
SPEND?

CHAPTER

06

UNDERSTANDING DEBT AND HOW TO MANAGEMENT IT

"Debt is like any other trap, easy enough to get into, but hard enough to get out of."

— Henry Wheeler Shaw.

Debt refers to borrowed money that must be repaid, usually with added interest. Common types of debt include credit card debt, student loans, car loans, and mortgages. While taking on debt can help you make large purchases, like a house or education, it can also become a heavy burden if you don't budget for how to repay it.

Debt had a grip on me more than once. Usually involving credit cards and not budgeting for the expense. I would simply buy what I wanted and figured I would pay it off over time without much consideration for the compounding interest or what I would sacrifice in my budget to cover the expense. I wasn't budgeting, so how could I account for the added expense?

Fast forward a few years, I started a business funded with credit cards. This in itself isn't necessarily a bad idea, but I had no budget in place on how to repay what I was spending. I was following the same pattern of credit card use that got me in trouble to begin with and was being eaten alive with debt, making minimum monthly payments, which wasn't enough to cover the monthly interest alone. I was just keeping my head above water but getting nowhere. The debt was growing, and I ended up filing for bankruptcy. This would be on my credit report for 7 years, affecting my credit score, my financial decisions, and interest rates on loans. The effect on credit score and interest rate is probably the most important takeaway. As we will discuss, interest is the most important factor in so many things we do. Most of us will not be paying cash for a house or car; we will finance it, and interest will be charged, which will be the number one impact on our monthly payment; the higher the rate, the higher the payment. This also directly impacts what we can buy. So, instead of getting a low interest rate, you are getting the highest rate possible, meaning you cannot afford to buy the top-of-the-line brand-new car. Instead, the only car that fits into your monthly budget with the high interest rate is the 10-year-old used vehicle with 100k miles.

Debt management is a critical aspect of personal finance that involves strategies to handle and repay debts efficiently. It requires an understanding of the types of debt, the impact of debt on financial health, and the best practices for managing and eliminating it. The true cost of debt is often underestimated because people don't consider how much interest adds up over time.

Understanding Interest: reference compound interest chapter

Interest is the cost of borrowing money. The longer it takes to repay your debt, the more interest you accrue. For example, if you take out a $10,000 loan at a 10% interest rate and make only minimum payments, you could end up paying significantly more in interest over the life of the loan than the original amount. This is why it's important to pay off debt as quickly as possible.

To see the effects of interest, here's a breakdown of payments for a $10,000 loan at a 10% annual compound interest rate over 60 months, with and without making extra payments.

Regular Payment Scenario

- **Monthly Payment**: $212.47
- **Total Paid Over 60 Months**: $12,748.23
- **Total Interest Paid**: $2,748.23
- **Loan Term**: 60 months

With an Extra $100 per Month

- **Monthly Payment (Including Extra $100)**: $312.47
- **Total Paid Over the Loan Term**: $11,679.70
- **Total Interest Paid**: $1,679.70

- **Loan Term**: 38 months

By adding an extra $100 per month to the monthly payment, the loan is paid off significantly faster—22 months earlier than the original 60-month term—and the total interest paid is reduced by $1,068.53 compared to the regular payment scenario. This demonstrates the powerful impact of making extra payments on reducing both the duration of the loan and the total cost of interest.

Compound Interest

Compound interest is one of the most impactful types of interest, as it can either grow your savings or dramatically increase your debt. We will discuss this in more detail in the next chapter, but just know it can exponentially increase your savings or investments. When it comes to debt, it can significantly increase the amount you owe, so it's important to manage debt wisely to avoid the negative impact of compounding.

The most important factor in determining the interest rate you get is your credit score. It affects your ability to get approved for loans, credit cards, and even housing. It determines if you get a low interest rate or high interest rate or if you get a loan at all. This, in turn, directly affects your financial health and your buying power.

The Importance of Understanding Your Debt

Before you can take control of your debt, it's important to fully understand the details. Many people take on loans or credit cards without fully grasping the long-term implications of interest rates, payment schedules, and other key factors.

Proper debt management is essential. It influences credit scores, financial freedom, and your overall financial stability. Mismanaged debt can lead to excessive interest payments, a damaged credit score, and possibly bankruptcy. Conversely, effectively managed debt can help in achieving financial goals, such as owning a home or car and pursuing education. I've lived through both of these scenarios, and believe me, the first is no fun. You are constantly chasing your tail, trying to make minimum payments to stay above water. Eventually, as it did to me, you sink.

Anytime you get a credit card or loan, pay attention to the interest rate and always stay within your budget. Everything goes back to your budget, so you need to get that right first.

Let's break down some of the key strategies to help you manage and pay off debt effectively.

Strategies for Paying Off Loans Effectively

Paying off loans effectively is crucial for financial health and can save you money on interest over time. Chances are, if you don't have a loan right now, you will at some point in your life. Here are some strategies to consider for efficiently managing and paying off your loans:

1. **Avalanche Method**: This strategy involves paying off loans with the highest interest rates first while maintaining minimum payments on others. This method minimizes the total interest paid over the life of your loans.
2. **Snowball Method**: This involves paying off your smallest debts first while making minimum payments on larger debts. Once the smallest debt is paid off, you move to the next smallest, creating a "snowball effect." This method can be motivating as you see loans being fully paid off.
3. **Consolidate Your Loans**: If managing multiple loans feels overwhelming, consider consolidating them into a single loan with a lower interest rate. This can simplify your payments, potentially reducing the amount of interest you pay and reducing your overall monthly expenses. This can be particularly effective for high-interest credit cards. If you can

get an introductory 0% interest rate on balance transfers and with a credit limit high enough to transfer your high-interest balances, you can lower your monthly payment and save a ton of money. The key is to pay it off during the introductory period. You also want to look at the fee. Credit cards usually charge a fee to transfer the balance. For me, the fee was worth it.

4. **Refinance**: Refinancing involves replacing an existing loan with a new one, typically at a lower interest rate. This can reduce your monthly payments and the total interest paid, which is especially useful for high-interest loans like private student loans, car loans, and home loans.

5. **Make Extra Payments**: Whenever possible, make more than the minimum payment. Making extra payments reduces your principal balance, which shortens the loan term and decreases total interest costs.

6. **Use Windfalls Wisely**: Apply any unexpected financial gains, such as tax refunds, bonuses, or inheritances, directly to your loan principal. This can reduce your balance more quickly than regular payments alone.

7. **Biweekly Payments**: Instead of monthly payments, consider biweekly payments. By paying half your monthly amount every two weeks, you'll make 26 half-payments or 13 full payments per year, which results in one extra full payment annually. This can shave months or even years off your loan term and save on interest.

8. **Budget Adjustments**: Review and adjust your budget to allocate more funds toward loan repayment. Cutting back on non-essential expenses can free up more money for paying down debts.

9. **Stay Informed**: Keep track of your loan terms, interest rates, and any fees associated with early payments. Under-

standing these details can help you plan the most effective payment strategy.

10. **Automate Your Payments**: Set up automatic payments to ensure you never miss a payment. This can sometimes lead to reduced interest rates, as some lenders offer a discount for automatic payments.

No one wants debt but for most, we are not going to be paying cash for every purchase. While debt can be a necessary tool, effective management is critical to minimizing its impact on your financial health. Implementing one or more of these strategies can help you manage your debt more effectively, reduce your debt quicker, and alleviate the financial stress associated with long-term debt. Before going to the next chapter take some time to go through the provided exercises and worksheets. Take a good look at your debt and map out a plan to get yourself out of it.

Debt Management Worksheets

Creating a comprehensive strategy for paying off loans requires careful planning and execution. Below, I'll outline a series of worksheets to guide you through reviewing your current debts and establishing a budget to effectively pay them off using various debt repayment strategies. These worksheets are designed to help you organize, prioritize, and strategize your loan repayments efficiently.

Worksheet 1: Debt Overview

This worksheet is your starting point for understanding and organizing your current debt situation.

Worksheet Format:

Loan Type	Total Amount Owed	Interest Rate	Minimum Monthly Payment	Due Date
Example: Credit Card	$5,000	18%	$150	15th
Example: Student Loan	$20,000	6%	$220	1st
Car Loan				
Personal Loan				
Total				

Instructions for Use:

- List all your debts, including credit cards, student loans, car loans, etc.
- Record the total amount owed, interest rate, minimum monthly payment, and due dates for each.
- Calculate the total of all minimum payments to understand your monthly debt obligation.

Worksheet 2: Debt Repayment Strategy Plan

Based on the strategies described, this worksheet helps you plan the method you will use to pay off your debts, whether it's the avalanche method, snowball method, or another strategy.

Worksheet Format:

Strategy	Description	Loan Type Targeted	Planned Extra Payment	Expected Payoff Time
Avalanche	Prioritize high-interest loans	Credit Card	$50	
Snowball	Prioritize smallest loans	Personal Loan	$50	

Consolidation	Combine loans for single payment	N/A	N/A	
Refinance	Secure lower interest rate	Car Loan	N/A	
Biweekly Payments	Increase payment frequency	Student Loan	See Calculation	

Instructions for Use:

- Choose a strategy for each loan based on what best fits your situation. You may use multiple strategies across different loans.
- Calculate how much extra you can pay toward targeted loans to speed up the payoff.
- Estimate how these strategies will change your payoff timeline.

Worksheet 3: Budget Adjustment for Loan Repayment

This worksheet helps you adjust your budget to find extra money for loan repayments.

Worksheet Format:

Category	Current Spending	Proposed Cut	Amount Redirected to Debt
Dining Out	$200	Reduce by 50%	$100
Entertainment	$150	Reduce by 30%	$45
Subscriptions	$100	Cancel unnecessary	$70
Total Redirected			$215

Instructions for Use:

- Review your monthly expenses to identify non-essential spending that can be reduced or eliminated.
- Decide how much you can realistically redirect from each category to increase your loan payments.
- Sum the amounts to calculate the total extra payment you can afford to make each month.

Exercises to Enhance Learning

Exercise 1: Interest Impact Analysis

- **Objective**: Visualize the impact of interest rates on the total cost of loans.
- **Action**: Use an online loan calculator to compare the total interest paid on your loans with and without extra payments.
- **Outcome**: Understand the financial benefit of increasing your loan payments.

Exercise 2: Windfall Allocation Plan

- **Objective**: Plan to use unexpected financial gains to pay down debt.
- **Action**: Decide in advance how any unexpected money (e.g., tax refunds, bonuses) will be distributed across your debts.
- **Outcome**: Prepare a strategy to maximize the impact of additional funds on your debt.

By utilizing these worksheets and engaging in the suggested exercises, you can gain a comprehensive understanding of your debt situation, strategically plan repayments, and adjust your budget to support faster debt reduction. These tools are designed to keep you organized and motivated throughout your debt-free journey.

Debt Repayment Strategy Comparison Worksheet

This worksheet is designed to compare the effectiveness of various debt repayment strategies based on your specific loans. It helps you evaluate each strategy side by side to make an informed decision about which to implement.

Worksheet Format:

Strategy	Target Debt	Interest Rate Before	Interest Rate After	Monthly Payment Before	Monthly Payment After	Total Interest Paid Before	Total Interest Paid After	Time to Payoff Before	Time to Payoff After	Notes
Avalanche	High-Interest									
Snowball	Smallest Debt									
Consolidation	Multiple									
Refinance	Specified Loan									
Bi-weekly	Any									
Extra Payments	Any									

Instructions for Use:

1. **Identify and List All Debts**: Start by listing all your debts in the rows under "Target Debt". Include information such as current interest rates and monthly payments.

2. **Apply Each Strategy**: For each row (strategy), calculate the effects if you applied that strategy to the debt:

- **Interest Rate After**: For consolidation and refinancing, note the new expected interest rate.
- **Monthly Payment After**: Determine what your new monthly payment would be under each strategy. For biweekly payments, calculate the total monthly cost by multiplying the biweekly payment by 2.167.
- **Total Interest Paid Before and After**: Use loan calculators to estimate the total interest paid over the life of the loan before and after applying the strategy.
- **Time to Payoff Before and After**: Calculate how long it will take to pay off the debt both before and after applying the strategy.

3. **Notes**: Make any relevant notes that might influence your decision, such as feasibility, impact on credit score, or personal preferences.

Outcome:

- This worksheet will provide a side-by-side comparison of how different strategies could affect your financial situation regarding each specific debt.
- Evaluate the results based on what is most important to you: lower payments, faster payoff, less interest paid, etc.

Additional Tips

- **Use Online Calculators**: For accurate calculations, especially for total interest and time to pay off, use online debt repayment calculators.
- **Consult Financial Advisors**: If you are unsure which strategy best suits your situation, consider consulting with a financial advisor who can provide personalized advice based on your overall financial picture.

- **Review Regularly**: Debt strategies may need adjustment as your financial situation changes, so review and update your worksheet regularly.

POOR
AVERAGE
GOOD
EXCELLENT
CREDIT SCORE

CHAPTER

07

THE IMPORTANCE OF CREDIT SCORES

"A credit score is not just a number; it's a reflection of your financial reputation."
— Suze Orman.

Understanding and managing one's credit score is an essential aspect of financial literacy that significantly impacts you financially, affecting everything from your ability to rent an apartment to the interest rate you receive on a mortgage or car loan and, ultimately, your budget. Yet, many people don't fully understand how their credit score is calculated or where this data comes from. Understanding the role of credit reporting agencies is a crucial part of managing and improving your credit score. Here, we explore why a good credit score is vital, how to manage and improve it, and the tools and strategies available to help.

A credit score was never a thought for me early on. I got a credit card when I first started college. Why they gave it to me, I'll never know, but I had it, used it, and couldn't pay it on time, much less pay it off. The interest was more than the minimum payment, and I eventually stopped paying for it. That wrecked my credit score. When I needed to get a car, my only credit line was the credit card that I didn't repay. So, of course, I had the highest interest rate imaginable for the car loan. The high interest rate meant higher monthly payments so I had to get less of a car. At this point, I started to realize the importance of a credit score. A high credit score will save you money and allow you to get more within your budget.

What Do Credit Reporting Agencies Do?

Credit scores are calculated based on information collected by credit reporting agencies (also known as credit bureaus). In the U.S., the three major credit reporting agencies are Equifax, Experian, and Transunion.

The primary role of these agencies is to collect and maintain data about your financial activities and share it with lenders, landlords, employers, and other entities that request access to your credit report. Almost everything you do financially is reported to the three major credit reporting agencies. Credit is looked at by employers, banks, insurance companies, and others to make a decision that will affect your financial situation. The importance of maintaining a good credit score cannot be overstated. Data included on your credit report includes:

- **Credit Accounts**: Information about your credit cards, loans, mortgages, and lines of credit. This includes account balances, credit limits, and payment history.
- **Payment History**: Whether or not you make your payments on time and how frequently you miss payments.
- **Credit Inquiries**: When a company or lender checks your credit, the inquiry is recorded. Too many inquiries in a short period can lower your score.
- **Public Records**: Information about bankruptcies, tax liens, or legal judgments that affect your financial standing.

Credit reporting agencies compile this data into a credit report, which is then used by credit scoring models (such as FICO and VantageScore) to calculate your credit score.

Components of a Credit Score

A credit score, which ranges from 300 to 850, is composed of five main components - payment history, amounts owed, length of credit history, credit mix, and new credit. Understanding the components of a credit score can empower you to manage it more effectively. Each of these components has a different weight on your overall score:

1. **Payment History (35%)**

This is the most significant factor affecting your credit score. It reflects whether you have paid past credit accounts on time. Late payments, bankruptcies, and other negative entries can significantly harm your score. Always make your payments on time. Almost nothing will damage your credit score more than late payments. Try setting up automatic payments so there is no chance of forgetting to make a payment. After years of forgetting and then having late payment fees added to the normal payment, I started doing this and just accounted for it in my budget. It is a lifesaver.

2. **Amounts Owed (30%)**

This factor considers the total amount of credit and loans you're using compared to your total credit limit, also known as your credit utilization ratio. High utilization can be a sign of financial distress and can lower your score.

Total balances are divided by total credit limits across all accounts. For example, if you have 2 credit cards with a total credit limit of $4,000 but have an outstanding balance of $2,000, then you would have a credit utilization ratio of 50%. You want to keep your credit utilization ratio below 30%.

3. **Length of Credit History (15%)**

Generally, a longer credit history will increase your score, as it provides more data on your spending habits and repayment behavior. Start establishing credit early. One effective way to get your credit history started in the right direction is with a secured credit card. A secured credit card is a great starting point if you have no credit history. It requires a cash deposit that serves as your credit limit. This minimizes the risk to the lender, making it easier to qualify for than an unsecured card. Start with your bank, see if they offer secured credit cards, and ask if they report the payments to the credit reporting agencies.

4. **Credit Mix (10%)**

This refers to the various credit types you manage (e.g., credit cards, installment loans, mortgages, etc.). A varied credit mix, such as a combination of credit cards, installment loans, and mortgages, can positively influence your credit score. For example, if you only have credit cards, then getting a mortgage may be more difficult because you haven't shown the ability to pay off a loan. An option here to show you can pay off a loan is to get a credit builder loan. These loans are offered by some credit unions and banks to help individuals build credit. The money you borrow is held in an account while you make payments. Your timely payments are reported to the credit bureaus, building your credit history.

5. **New Credit (10%)**

Opening several new credit accounts in a short period can represent greater risk, especially for people who don't have a long credit history. This includes hard inquiries made when lenders check your credit before giving you a loan or credit card. Hard inquiries - performed when applying for credit - temporarily reduce your credit score. In the past, when looking for a loan, I would go to one car dealer after another, letting them pull my credit report without thinking about what it was doing to my credit score. This affects the interest rate, there can be a huge difference between the rate for having a score of 700 versus 699. Now, I go to my credit union, get approved for the loan, know my interest rate, and then shop for a car. I know how much I can spend and only have one hard credit inquiry.

Why is a Good Credit Score Important?

As mentioned earlier in my experience with my first credit card and then trying to buy a car, a good credit score can affect several areas of your life, including how you budget:

1. **Loan and Credit Card Approvals**: Lenders are likelier to approve applicants with good credit scores for loans and credit cards at more favorable interest rates.

2. **Lower Interest Rates**: Higher scores often result in lower interest rates on loans and credit cards, meaning lower overall borrowing costs.

3. **Rental Houses and Apartments**: Landlords may check credit scores before renting. A higher score can make it easier to secure a rental.

4. **Utility Services**: Utility companies may require a security deposit if you have a low credit score. A good score can eliminate this need.

5. **Job Opportunities**: Some employers check credit scores as part of the application process, particularly for positions that require financial responsibility.

A credit score isn't just a number. It directly affects your buying power. The higher the rate, the higher the payment, meaning you can buy less. Less car, less house, less everything.

Techniques to Manage and Improve Credit Scores

1. **Regularly Check Credit Reports**: Obtain a free copy of your credit report from each of the three major credit reporting agencies (Equifax, Experian, and TransUnion) once a year. Check for errors and dispute any inaccuracies.

2. **Pay Bills on Time**: Late payments can have a significant negative impact on your credit score. Setting up automatic payments or reminders can help ensure bills are paid on time.

3. **Reduce Credit Card Balances**: High outstanding debt can affect a credit score. Aim to keep your credit card balances well below your credit limits.

4. **Limit New Credit Applications**: Each time you apply for credit, a hard inquiry is made, which can lower your score. Limit applications for new credit and only apply when necessary.

5. **Keep Your Credit Utilization Below 30%**: Track how much of your available credit you're using. Keep your balances low to maintain a good credit score. High credit utilization can signal financial instability to lenders. Aim to use less than 30% of your available credit.

6. **Diversify Your Credit Mix**: Use a combination of credit products like credit cards, student loans, and car loans to build a healthy credit profile. Lenders like to see that you can manage various types of credit responsibly. It accounts for 10% of your score.

Why Do You Need to Monitor All Three Reports?

Although each of the three agencies collects similar data, their information on file may differ slightly. Not all creditors report to all three bureaus, so information may vary across your reports. For instance, one credit card company may report to Equifax and Experian but not to TransUnion. Therefore, your credit score may vary slightly between the agencies. It's important to monitor your credit report from each bureau to ensure all the information is accurate and up to date.

Common Differences Between Credit Reports:

- **Credit inquiries**: Different lenders may pull your credit from different agencies, which means a hard inquiry might show up on one report but not on the others.
- **Account details**: A loan or credit card might be reported to one agency but not the others.
- **Errors or inconsistencies**: Mistakes such as outdated or incorrect information can appear on one report but not others, so it's crucial to check all three.

How to Access Your Credit Reports from the Three Agencies

Each year, you are entitled to one free credit report from each of the three major bureaus. There are many different options when it comes to accessing your credit reports. I use the ones offered by my credit card. Most offer free credit monitoring. The credit monitoring services offered typically alert you to changes in your credit report, such as new accounts opened in your name, changes to your credit limits, or significant balance changes. These alerts can help you quickly detect potential fraud or errors on your credit report. I like this option because it is free and because it is ongoing, and I can see my credit report at any time. Another option is to go to **AnnualCreditReport.com.** This is the official website authorized by the federal government to provide free credit reports. You can request reports from Equifax, Experian, and TransUnion once per year. Once you have the report, you want to:

1. Review the reports carefully for any errors or discrepancies. Common mistakes include incorrect payment history, wrong account balances, or accounts that don't belong to you.
2. Dispute any errors found directly with the credit reporting agency. Each agency has an online dispute process that allows you to provide evidence and request a correction.

Budget Tool Resources for Credit Management

1. **Mint**: This tool not only helps with budgeting but also offers credit score monitoring, providing insights into what affects your score and how to improve it.
2. **Credit Karma**: Provides free access to your credit scores, reports, and monitoring. Credit Karma also educates users on factors affecting their scores and offers personalized advice.
3. **Experian Boost**: A free service that allows you to increase your credit score by getting credit for your utility and phone bill payments.
4. **Credit Cards:** Many credit cards provide free credit monitoring services, offering alerts for inquiries, score changes, and tips to improve your credit.

Understanding and managing your credit score is a crucial component of financial literacy that impacts many areas of life.

By responsibly managing credit, regularly reviewing credit reports, and engaging in targeted exercises to improve credit health, individuals can enhance their financial well-being, gain access to better borrowing terms, and achieve greater financial flexibility and security. Remember, a low score means a higher interest rate, higher payments, and less buying power. Your budget is your budget; your credit will determine what fits in your budget. Meaning, do you get a 4 bedroom 3 bath house or a 2 bedroom one 1 bath home? Both could be within your budget, depending on your credit score.

2 0 2 5
4

CHAPTER

08

UNDERSTANDING SAVING AND INVESTING

"The quickest way to double your money is to fold it in half and put it in your back pocket."
— Will Rogers.

Saving is important, but **investing** is what enables your money to grow and work on your behalf. While investing can initially seem intimidating, you don't need to be an expert to start. The earlier you begin investing, the more you benefit from **compound interest**, which allows your money to earn interest on interest over time.

What is Compound Interest?

One of the most powerful yet underappreciated concepts in personal finance is compound interest. The earlier you understand it, the more time you have to benefit from it. But what exactly is compound interest, and how can you make it work for you?

Simply put, compound interest occurs when the interest earned on your savings or investments begins to generate its own interest, leading to exponential growth over time. The key is starting early. The more time your money has to compound, the faster it grows.

For example, let's say you start saving $100 a month in a retirement account that earns a 6% annual interest rate. If you start at age 25 and continue until you retire at 65, you'll have nearly $200,000. If you wait until age 35 to start saving the same amount, you'll only have about $100,000 by the time you retire. That's a difference of $100,000 just because of a 10-year delay in starting your savings!

This simple yet powerful concept is often overlooked by young adults, who may think they have plenty of time to start saving later. But the earlier you begin, the more profound the impact of compound interest.

I remember when I was in my early twenties, I had just started my first job and was excited about finally earning a steady income. However, I was more focused on spending my money on experiences—going out with friends, traveling, and buying the latest gadgets. Saving and investing were the last things on my mind. I thought, "I'm young; I'll start saving later when I make more money."

Years later, I learned about compound interest. I realized that by not saving even a little bit in my early twenties, I had missed out on years of potential growth. It was a tough pill to swallow, but it pushed me to start investing immediately. And while I had lost some time, the important thing was that I started. It's never too late to let compound interest work for you, but the earlier you start, the better.

Harnessing Compound Interest:

Harnessing the power of compound interest is one of the most effective ways to grow your savings over time and significantly increase your wealth, especially over long periods. Here are strategies to maximize the benefits of compound interest:

1. **Start Early**: The sooner you begin saving, the more time compound interest has to accelerate your money's growth. Even small amounts can grow significantly over decades.

2. **Regular Contributions**: Consistently add to your savings. Regular contributions, even if they are small, can have a big impact due to compound interest. Consider setting up automatic transfers to a savings account right after you receive your paycheck.

3. **Reinvest Earnings**: Allow your interest earnings to be reinvested rather than removed. This practice increases the principal amount on which future interest is calculated, accelerating the growth of your savings.

4. **Use High-Interest Savings Accounts**: Place your savings in high-yield accounts or certificates of deposit (CDs) that offer higher interest rates than regular savings accounts. Research and compare rates from different financial institutions to find the best option.

5. **Invest in Stocks or Mutual Funds**: For long-term savings, consider investing in the stock market or mutual funds. These can offer higher returns than traditional savings accounts, albeit with higher risks. Dividend-paying stocks can be particularly powerful as dividends can be reinvested to purchase more shares, further compounding your investment.

6. **Maximize Retirement Contributions**: Take full advantage of retirement accounts like 401(k)s or IRAs, which benefit from tax-deferred or tax-free growth, enhancing the compounding effect. If possible, contribute the maximum amount allowable to these accounts.

7. **Utilize Matching Contributions**: If your employer offers a matching contribution on your 401(k) or another retirement plan, make sure to contribute at least enough to get the maximum match. This is essentially free money that will also benefit from compound interest.

8. **Avoid Early Withdrawals**: Withdrawing funds early from savings or investment accounts can significantly diminish the power of compound interest, as you lose out on future earning potential. Avoid dipping into these funds unless absolutely necessary.

9. **Be Patient**: Compounding works best over time. The longer your money remains invested or in a savings account, the more significant the compound effects will be.

10. **Monitor and Adjust**: Regularly review your savings and investment strategies to ensure they align with your financial goals and take advantage of the best available interest rates and investment opportunities.

By employing these strategies, you can effectively utilize compound interest to build a substantial financial reserve, providing you with greater security and the potential for financial independence in the future.

Understand Risk vs. Reward

All investments involve some level of risk, but higher-risk investments often provide the potential for greater returns. It's important to find a balance between risk and reward based on your comfort level and financial goals.

- **Low-Risk Investments**: Bonds and savings accounts are generally considered low-risk. While they offer lower returns, they provide more stability and safety.
- **High-Risk Investments**: Stocks and mutual funds tend to have higher returns, but they also come with more volatility. It's essential to have a long-term view of these investments to ride out market fluctuations.

For me, when I started investing, it was later in life. I felt I needed to catch up so I put my money in high-risk investments. I knew I would not be withdrawing the money anytime soon and was content with riding the ups and downs of the market. At my job, I did the same. My 401(k) investments I chose were high-risk and I made sure I got the full employer match. If I had started early in life, I would most likely pick high-risk as well because, again, you are playing the long game. High risk isn't necessary; you just need to start early.

Retirement Planning in Your 20s: Why It's Essential

It may seem early to think about retirement when you're in your 20s, but starting now can make a significant difference. By contributing to retirement accounts early on, you take advantage of compound interest growth over decades.

1. **The Benefits of Starting Early**

The earlier you start saving for retirement, the more time your money has to grow. Even small contributions can add up significantly over time due to the power of compound interest.

Example:

If Mia starts contributing $200 per month to her 401(k) at age 25, by the time she's 65, she will have contributed $96,000, but her account could grow to over $500,000, assuming an average 7% annual return. If Mia waits until she's 35 to start saving the same amount, her account would only grow to about $245,000 by age 65.

2. **Choosing the Right Retirement Accounts**

Understanding the various types of retirement savings options, such as 401(k) plans and Individual Retirement Accounts (IRAs), is essential for effective retirement planning. These vehicles offer unique benefits, tax advantages, and rules that can significantly impact your financial future. Below, we delve deeper into these types of retirement accounts, along with budgeting techniques and tools that can help maximize their potential.

Detailed Overview of 401(k) Plans and IRAs

401(k) Plans

A 401(k) plan is a tax-advantaged, employer-sponsored retirement savings plan. Employees can contribute a portion of their salary on a pre-tax basis, which lowers their taxable income. Many employers offer a matching contribution, which can significantly enhance an employee's retirement savings. It's important to make sure you tax advantage of the employer match. For example, a 5% employer 401k match means that if you contribute 5% of your salary to your 401k, your employer will contribute an equal amount, also 5% of your salary, to your retirement account, essentially "matching" your contribution dollar-for-dollar up to that 5% limit. If you earn $50,000 per year and contribute 5% to your 401k, which would be $2,500, your employer would also contribute $2,500, giving you a total contribution of $5,000 to your retirement account. Free money!

- **Types of 401(k) Plans:**
    - Traditional 401(k): Contributions are made with pre-tax dollars, reducing taxable income. Taxes are paid when withdrawals are made in retirement.
    - Roth 401(k): Contributions are made with after-tax dollars, and withdrawals in retirement are tax-free, provided certain conditions are met.
- **Contribution Limits:** For 2023, the contribution limit for employees is $22,500, with an additional **catch-up contribution of $7,500 for those aged 50 and older.** This limit may can change from year to year so always check with your employer or the IRS for current information.
- **Benefits:** Tax-deferred growth of investments and potential employer-matching contributions enhance the growth potential of your retirement funds.

Individual Retirement Accounts (IRAs)

IRAs are personal retirement savings plans available to anyone with earned income. They offer tax advantages that help your savings grow more efficiently.

- **Types of IRAs:**
    - **Traditional IRA:** Contributions may be tax-deductible, and the investments grow tax-deferred. Taxes are paid on withdrawals in retirement.
    - **Roth IRA:** Contributions are made with after-tax money, and earnings can be withdrawn tax-free in retirement under certain conditions.
    - **SEP IRA:** Designed for self-employed individuals and small business owners. Offers higher contribution limits compared to traditional and Roth IRAs.

- **Contribution Limits:** For 2023, the total contributions for Traditional and Roth IRAs are limited to $6,500 or $7,500 if you're age 50 or older.
- **Benefits:** Flexible investment choices and potential for tax-free growth or tax deductions depending on the type of IRA.

Budgeting Techniques to Maximize Retirement Contributions

1. **Prioritize Retirement Savings:** Treat retirement contributions like a regular expense in your budget. Ensure you contribute enough to capture any employer match, as this is essentially free money.
2. **Automate Contributions:** Set up automatic transfers to your retirement accounts to ensure consistent savings. This also helps in budgeting as you adjust your monthly expenses based on what's left after savings.
3. **Use Windfalls Wisely:** Allocate a portion of any windfalls, such as bonuses or tax refunds, directly into your retirement savings accounts to boost your balance without impacting your regular budget.

Budget Tool Resources

1. **Vanguard Retirement Nest Egg Calculator:** This helps you estimate how long your retirement savings might last based on your spending and savings balance.
2. **IRA Contribution Calculator (Bankrate):** A tool to help determine how much you can contribute to an IRA each year based on your income, filing status, and other retirement plans.
3. **Bloomberg's 401(k) Savings Calculator:** Estimates your retirement savings balance and withdrawals for any 401(k) plan.

3. **How Much Should You Save for Retirement?**

Financial experts generally recommend saving at least 15% of your pre-tax income for retirement. However, if you can't save that much yet, don't worry—start with what you can and gradually increase your contributions over time.

Example:

John's employer offers a 401(k) with a 5% match. He earns $50,000 per year, so by contributing 5% ($2,500), he gets an additional $2,500 from his employer. This $5,000 annual contribution grows tax-free, setting him up for a secure retirement.

One of the easiest ways to build wealth and secure your financial future is to automate your savings. When you automate your savings, you ensure that a portion of your income goes directly into your savings or investment accounts without you having to think about it. This removes the temptation to spend that money, making saving consistent and effortless.

What is Automated Savings?

Automated savings is the process of setting up recurring transfers from your checking account to a savings or investment account. This could be a retirement account like a 401(k), an emergency fund, or a brokerage account for long-term investments. By automating your savings, you eliminate the need for willpower and make saving a habit.

Real-Life Example:

Mark and Steve both earn $3,000 a month. Mark manually transfers money to his savings when he remembers or feels like it, while Steve has set up an automatic transfer of $300 each month to his savings account. After a year, Steve has $3,600 saved, while Mark has less than $1,000 because he frequently forgets to save or spends the money on other things. Automating savings ensures consistency and prevents the temptation to spend the money instead.

I used to struggle with saving consistently. I would tell myself that I would put money into my savings account at the end of the month, but more often than not, something would come up—an unexpected bill, a night out with friends—and my savings would take a back seat. Once I set up an automatic transfer that moved money into my savings account the day after payday, everything changed. I didn't even miss the money because it was out of sight and out of mind. Within a year, I had built up a savings buffer that gave me a sense of financial security I'd never had before.

Budget is the key work here. As we have been saying throughout this book, you have to budget. If savings is part of your budget and you automate the savings, you will never miss the money because you planned to not have it to spend.

Worksheet for Compound Interest Exploration

Objective: Visualize the effect of compound interest on investments over various periods and with different contributions.

Worksheet Structure:

Initial Investment	Monthly Contribution	Annual Interest Rate	Compounding Frequency	Years of Investment	Future Value
$5,000	$100	5%	Annually	10	[Calculated]
$5,000	$100	5%	Monthly	10	[Calculated]
$5,000	$100	7%	Annually	10	[Calculated]
[Add more rows as needed]					

Instructions:

1. Enter various scenarios by changing initial investments, monthly contributions, interest rates, compounding frequencies, and investment durations.
2. Leverage an online compound interest calculator to estimate the future value for each scenario.
3. Analyze how adjusting each variable impacts the total accumulation of your investments.

Outcome:

- Develop a clear understanding of how different factors affect the growth of investments over time.

Worksheet for Investment Strategy Planning

Objective: Develop a realistic and achievable investment plan utilizing compound interest to meet specific financial goals.

Worksheet Structure:

Financial Goal	Target Amount	Current Savings	Years to Goal	Estimated Annual Return	Monthly Contribution Needed
Retirement	$500,000	$50,000	20	6%	[Calculated]
College Fund	$100,000	$10,000	10	4%	[Calculated]
[Add more rows as needed]					

Instructions:

1. Define each of your financial goals.
2. Input your target amount, current savings, desired timeline, and expected return rate.

3. Calculate the monthly contribution needed using a financial calculator.

4. Adjust your plan based on the feasibility of these contributions.

Outcome:

- Create a detailed, personalized investment plan that clearly outlines steps to achieve your financial objectives.

Worksheet for Interest Rate Sensitivity Analysis

Objective: Analyze the sensitivity of your investment outcomes to changes in interest rates.

Worksheet Structure:

Interest Rate Scenario	Initial Investment	Monthly Contribution	Years of Investment	Future Value
3%	$10,000	$200	15	[Calculated]
5%	$10,000	$200	15	[Calculated]
7%	$10,000	$200	15	[Calculated]
[Add more rows as needed]				

Instructions:

1. Set a consistent initial investment, monthly contribution, and investment duration.

2. Apply different interest rate scenarios to see how they affect the future value of the investment.

3. Use a financial calculator to determine the future values and record them in the worksheet.

Outcome:

- Understand how fluctuating interest rates can impact your investment returns and plan accordingly to mitigate risks.

CHAPTER

09

CREATING MULTIPLE INCOME STREAMS FOR FINANCIAL INDEPENDENCE

"Financial fitness is not a pipe dream or a state of mind. It's a reality if you are willing to pursue it and embrace it."
— Will Robinson.

The pursuit of financial independence is often directly linked to the ability to create and sustain multiple income streams. By diversifying income sources, individuals can build financial resilience, decrease dependence on a single source of earnings, and accelerate their path to financial freedom.

We all want financial freedom. That is the ultimate, right? Buy what we want when we want without a thought to the cost. Never worry about a budget, savings, or an emergency fund. Just an endless stream of money to spend as we please. We all probably have different views on what financial independence looks like. For some, it may mean being able to pay all of your bills and having enough to go on a vacation once a year. For others, it may mean having zero debt. Whatever it looks like for you, it is obtainable. There are so many ways these days to make additional income, from starting a lawn care service on the side to being a social media influencer. The key is multiple income streams. The days of one income stream are dead.

It will explore the significance of multiple income streams, provide real-world examples, introduce techniques and tools for achieving financial independence, and suggest exercises to enhance understanding and application.

Importance of Multiple Income Streams

1. **Risk Mitigation**: Relying on a single income source can be risky. If that source is compromised (e.g., through job loss or industry downturn), financial stability can be threatened. Multiple income streams protect against this risk, providing safety nets that can sustain you through economic fluctuations.

2. **Accelerated Wealth Building**: Multiple income streams can exponentially increase your savings rate, allowing for faster wealth accumulation and earlier achievement of financial goals, such as retirement.

3. **Enhanced Financial Flexibility**: With more income comes more options for investing, spending, and saving. This flexibility allows you to make choices that can further secure your financial future, such as investing in higher-return assets or purchasing insurance products.

Real-World Examples

1. **Sarah's Consulting Firm**: Sarah, a marketing professional, started a side consulting business alongside her corporate job. This not only provided her with extra income but also allowed her to build a client base that made her transition to full-time self-employment smoother and financially safer.

2. **Tom's Rental Properties**: After reading about real estate investments, Tom purchased a duplex to rent out. The rental income now covers all his property-related expenses and generates profit, contributing significantly to his income.

3. **Linda's Online Course**: Linda, a graphic designer, created an online course about design fundamentals. This course now serves as a passive income stream, complementing her income from freelance projects and her part-time job at a design firm.

Techniques to Achieve Financial Independence

Creating multiple income streams is a powerful strategy for achieving financial independence. Diversifying your income can provide security, reduce financial stress from any single source, and accelerate your path to financial freedom. Here's a step-by-step guide on how to develop multiple income streams:

1. Assess Your Skills and Resources

Start by evaluating your skills, interests, and resources. Consider what you're good at, what you enjoy, and what unique resources or assets you can leverage. This could include professional skills, hobbies, or items you own that can be turned into income sources.

2. **Diversify Your Employment Income**

- **Freelancing**: Use your professional skills to take on freelance work. Platforms like Upwork, Freelancer, or industry-specific job boards can help you find gigs.

- **Part-Time Job**: Depending on your time availability, a part-time job in a field you enjoy can supplement your primary income.

3. **Invest in Real Estate**

- **Rental Properties**: Investing in property that you can rent out can provide a steady source of passive income. Consider both residential and commercial properties.

- **Real Estate Investment Trusts (REITs)**: If direct property management isn't appealing, REITs offer a way to invest in real estate without buying or managing the property yourself.

4. **Create Passive Income Streams**

- **Dividend Stocks**: Invest in dividend-paying stocks to receive regular payouts from your investments.

- **Create Digital Products**: Write eBooks, develop online courses, or create apps that provide ongoing income after the initial creation effort.

5. **Leverage the Gig Economy**

- **Rideshare Driving**: Platforms like Uber or Lyft can provide flexible income based on your schedule.

- **Delivery Services**: Work for food or package delivery services whenever you have spare time.

6. **Start a Side Business**

- **E-commerce**: Sell products online through platforms like Etsy, eBay, or Amazon.
- **Crafting or Art**: Turn your creative talents into a business by selling your creations online or at local markets.

7. **Invest Wisely**

- **Stock Market**: Besides dividend stocks, consider broad-market index funds or ETFs which can grow over time.
- **Peer-to-Peer Lending**: Platforms like LendingClub or Prosper allow you to lend money to individuals in small increments, earning interest as they repay their loans.

8. **Utilize Technology and Automation**

- **Robo-Advisors**: Use technology for investment management to optimize your returns with minimal effort.
- **Automate Savings**: Set up automatic transfers to savings accounts or investment portfolios to consistently build wealth.

9. **Build an Online Presence**

- **Blogging or Vlogging**: Monetize your expertise or interests through advertising, sponsorships, or affiliate marketing on your blog or YouTube channel.

10. **Continuous Learning and Adaptation**

- **Stay Updated**: Keep learning about new opportunities and ways to monetize your interests and skills.
- **Networking**: Engage with others in your fields of interest to find new opportunities and collaborative ventures.

By combining several of these strategies, you can build a robust financial foundation that not only covers your expenses but also grows over time, moving you closer to financial independence. Remember, the key is to start small, be consistent, and gradually expand your efforts as you gain more experience and stability in each area. Don't forget to budget. Starting a side hustle may require an initial investment, so make sure you budget for that cost.

Creating multiple income streams is a powerful strategy for securing financial independence. By diversifying your sources of income, you enhance your financial stability, increase your wealth-building capacity, and provide yourself with various financial options. Implementing the discussed techniques, using the recommended tools, and actively engaging in the provided exercises can significantly boost your ability to achieve and maintain financial independence.

My Goals
Financial
Independence

CHAPTER

10

UNDERSTANDING AND IMPLEMENTING FINANCIAL GOALS

Setting and achieving financial goals can be challenging for many, including myself. I always start out strong, with goals in mind, trying to follow through, but I never really had a structured way to stay on track. So, I end up just trying to keep track in my head or by writing down an expense on random pieces of paper, thinking I will remember. Of course, none of this worked. These are not techniques or a sustainable way to set and implement financial goals.

Well-defined financial goals provide direction for how you manage your money, influencing both your saving and spending habits. Even more important than setting and prioritizing financial goals is knowing how to keep track of your goals.

Importance of Financial Goals

Financial goals are the specific objectives or benchmarks you set to guide your financial decisions and track your progress. Whether saving for retirement, buying a home, or simply managing daily expenses more efficiently, having clear goals can help you prioritize your resources effectively and make strategic decisions that align with your long-term aspirations.

Examples of Financial Goals

1. **Emergency Fund**: Anna, a freelance graphic designer, sets a goal to save six months' worth of living expenses to buffer against periods of unstable income. Within two years, she achieves this by setting aside 10% of every payment she receives.

2. **Debt-Free Living**: John, burdened with student loans and credit card debt, sets a goal to be debt-free within five years. He prioritizes his high-interest debt and refinances some of his loans to achieve this goal ahead of schedule.

3. **Retirement**: Lisa, in her mid-30s, starts late on her retirement planning. She sets a goal to maximize her retirement

contributions to catch up and takes advantage of her company's 401(k) match program, aiming to retire comfortably.

4. **Education Fund**: The Chen family plans to send their two children to college without the burden of student loans. They set up a 529 College Savings Plan when their children are young, contributing monthly to meet their goal by the time their kids are college-age.

Techniques for Setting Financial Goals

To ensure that financial goals are effective and motivating, it's important to employ robust planning techniques. These methods help in translating vague aspirations into actionable plans. Below, we'll delve deeper into three essential techniques for setting financial goals: SMART Goals, Prioritizing Goals, and Incremental Milestones. We'll explore how each can be used to structure and refine your financial planning process.

1. **SMART Goals**

Specific, Measurable, Achievable, Relevant, and Time-bound (SMART) goals are a foundation in goal-setting theory that can be particularly effective in financial planning:

- **Specific**: Goals should be clear and specific to avoid ambiguity. For example, instead of saying, "I want to save more money," specify, "I want to save $5,000."
- **Measurable**: You should be able to track your progress towards the goal. In financial terms, this means setting a dollar amount or a percentage that can be quantified, like saving 10% of your monthly income. So if you make $4,000 per month you would save $400 per month towards the $5,000 goal.
- **Achievable**: While ambition is important, your goals also need to be realistic and attainable to keep you motivated.

For example, if you're earning $50,000 a year, setting a goal to save $1 million in a year isn't achievable.

- **Relevant**: Ensure that your financial goals align with your broader life goals and current financial situation. For instance, if you plan to buy a home, your financial goals should include saving for a down payment.

- **Time-bound**: Every goal needs a clearly defined timeline. Setting a deadline, like saving for a vacation in 12 months, creates a sense of urgency and can help you stay focused and motivated.

Example: Emily sets a SMART goal to pay off her $10,000 credit card debt in 24 months. She plans to do this by paying $417 monthly, aligning this goal with her broader objective of improving her credit score to purchase a home.

2. **Prioritizing Goals**

Financial resources are often limited, making it crucial to prioritize goals based on urgency and importance:

- **Immediate Needs vs. Future Wants**: Distinguish between what you need now (such as paying off high-interest debt) and what you want in the future (like a dream vacation or luxury purchase).

- **High Impact vs. Low Impact**: Some goals will significantly impact your financial health (like saving for retirement), while others might be less impactful but still important to your personal satisfaction (such as remodeling a kitchen).

- **Sequential Prioritization**: Some goals naturally precede others. For example, building an emergency fund is advisable before investing in stocks or other less liquid assets.

Example: John categorizes his goals into tiers: Tier 1 includes building an emergency fund and paying off credit card debt, Tier 2 focuses on saving for a down payment on a house, and

Tier 3 covers long-term objectives like retirement savings and college funds for his kids.

3. **Incremental Milestones**

Dividing significant financial goals into smaller, achievable milestones makes the process more manageable and less overwhelming:

- **Short-Term Milestones**: These are immediate steps that can be achieved quickly, such as saving $1,000 in an emergency fund over the next three months.
- **Medium-Term Milestones**: These goals take a bit longer and build upon short-term achievements, such as increasing that emergency fund to $5,000 within a year.
- **Long-Term Milestones**: These are the ultimate objectives that short-term and medium-term goals build toward, like saving $500,000 for retirement.

Example: Linda's goal is to save $20,000 for a new car in four years. She sets up milestones of saving $5,000 each year, monitoring her progress through her budgeting app, and adjusting her savings plan annually based on her success in meeting these yearly goals.

Financial Goals Tool Resources

1. **Mint**: This app helps track your spending against your budgets and financial goals, providing alerts and insights to keep you on track.
2. **YNAB (You Need A Budget)**: YNAB focuses on giving every dollar a job, helping users allocate funds towards various financial goals efficiently.
3. **Personal Capital**: Offers tools for tracking and managing your investments, calculating your net worth, and planning for retirement.

Setting and prioritizing financial goals not only gives direction to your saving and spending but also empowers you to achieve the best possible financial health and readiness for the future. By employing the described techniques, tools, and exercises, you can enhance your understanding and effectiveness in managing your finances, thus paving the way toward realizing your financial aspirations.

To assist you in managing and planning your retirement savings more effectively, I have created three detailed worksheets based on the budgeting exercises provided. These worksheets are designed to help you visualize your retirement planning, identify potential savings from your current expenses, and review your investment allocations. You can create these worksheets in a digital spreadsheet program like Microsoft Excel or Google Sheets, which will allow for easy calculations and adjustments.

Worksheet 1: Retirement Planning Exercise

This worksheet is designed to help you calculate and project your retirement savings based on your current age, retirement age, current savings, monthly contributions, and expected rate of return.

Worksheet Format:

Current Age	Retirement Age	Current Retirement Savings	Monthly Contributions	Expected Rate of Return	Estimated Retirement Savings at Retirement
30	65	$50,000	$500	6%	[Calculated]
[Add row]	[Add row]	[Add row]	[Add row]	[Add row]	[Add row]

Instructions for Use:

1. Fill in your current age, desired retirement age, current retirement savings, monthly contributions, and the expected rate of return.
2. Use an online compound interest calculator to estimate the future value of your retirement savings.
3. Adjust the monthly contributions to see how changes affect the final retirement savings.

Outcome:

- Understand how your current savings habits will impact your financial status at retirement and make necessary adjustments to meet your goals.

Worksheet 2: Expense Reduction Exercise

This worksheet helps you analyze your monthly spending and identify potential savings by reducing non-essential expenses, which can then be redirected to enhance your retirement savings.

Worksheet Format:

Expense Category	Monthly Spending	Potential Savings	Additional Monthly Contribution to Retirement
Dining Out	$250	$125	$125
Entertainment	$150	$75	$75
[Add row]	[Add row]	[Add row]	[Add row]

Instructions for Use:

1. Document all non-essential monthly expenses.
2. Determine potential savings by reducing these expenses.

3. Calculate how much of the savings you can reallocate to your retirement contributions.

Outcome:

- Optimize your spending habits to increase contributions to your retirement savings, accelerating your progress toward financial independence.

Worksheet 3: Investment Allocation Review

This worksheet is designed for you to review and potentially adjust your investment allocations within your retirement portfolio to better align with your age and risk tolerance.

Worksheet Format:

Investment Type	Percentage of Portfolio	Performance (3-Year Average)	Adjusted Allocation
Stocks	60%	8%	[Calculated]
Bonds	40%	3%	[Calculated]
[Add row]	[Add row]	[Add row]	[Add row]

Instructions for Use:

1. List all investment types within your retirement accounts.
2. Note the current percentage of your total portfolio each type represents.
3. Review their performance and consult with a financial advisor to determine the ideal allocation based on your current age and risk tolerance.

Outcome:

- Achieve an optimized investment portfolio that balances growth potential with appropriate risk management tailored to your retirement planning needs.

Implementation Tips

- **Regularly Update**: Review and update these worksheets periodically to reflect changes in your financial situation, market conditions, or personal goals.
- **Seek Professional Advice**: Consider consulting with a financial advisor to discuss your findings and get professional input on your investment strategies and retirement planning.
- **Digital Tracking**: Utilize digital tools to maintain and calculate your worksheets efficiently, allowing for dynamic updates and projections.

Worksheet 1: Goal Visualization Exercise

This worksheet is designed to help you visualize your financial goals, making them more tangible and motivating.

Worksheet Format:

Goal Description	Category (Short/Medium/Long-Term)	Amount Needed	Deadline	Visual Representation (Link or Description)
Example: Save for a new car	Short-Term	$20,000	Dec 2024	[Insert Image/ Chart]
Example: Pay off student loans	Medium-Term	$35,000	Dec 2026	[Insert Image/ Chart]
[Add more rows as needed]				

Instructions for Use:

1. List all your financial goals.
2. Categorize each goal as short-term, medium-term, or long-term.

3. Define the amount needed and establish a realistic deadline for each goal.

4. Add a visual representation such as a chart, graph, or image that you can refer to. Use digital tools like Canva to create visuals or simply describe the visual concept.

5. Place this worksheet where you can see it daily, or use a digital version as your desktop wallpaper.

Outcome:

- A clear, visual tool that keeps your financial goals at the forefront of your daily activities, enhancing motivation and focus.

Worksheet 2: Budgeting for Goals

This worksheet integrates your financial goals into your monthly budget, ensuring that you allocate funds to achieve these goals systematically.

Worksheet Format:

Month	Total Income	Essential Expenses	Goal Contributions	Remaining Balance	Notes
Example: January	$3,000	$2,000	$500	$500	Adjust next month's contribution
[Add more rows for each month]					

Instructions for Use:

1. Record your total monthly income.

2. List your essential expenses (rent, utilities, food, etc.).

3. Allocate a specific amount to your prioritized financial goals.
4. Calculate the remaining balance after essential expenses and goal contributions.
5. Make notes for any adjustments needed in the next budget cycle.

Outcome:

- A structured approach to ensure your budget aligns with achieving your financial goals, with clear visibility into where adjustments are needed.

Worksheet 3: Goal Progress Review Sessions

This worksheet facilitates regular reviews of your financial goals to ensure they remain aligned with your changing financial circumstances.

Worksheet Format:

Review Date	Goal	Progress	Adjustments Needed	Next Review Date	Notes
Example: 2024-Q1	Retirement Savings	On track	Increase monthly contribution	2024-Q2	Invest in higher yield account
[Add more rows for each session]					

Instructions for Use:

1. Schedule and note the date of each review session.
2. Evaluate the progress made towards each goal.
3. Identify any adjustments needed to stay on track or to respond to changes in your financial situation.

4. Set the next review date and make notes on specific focus areas for the next period.

Outcome:

- Ensures continuous monitoring and adjustment of your financial plans, adapting to life changes, and improving the likelihood of achieving your goals.

SMART Goals Worksheet

Objective: Define and detail each financial goal using the SMART criteria to ensure goals are actionable and aligned with personal aspirations.

Worksheet Structure:

Goal Description	Specific	Measurable	Achievable	Relevant	Time-bound
Example: Save for a down payment	Save $20,000 for a home down payment	Track progress through monthly savings	Save $500 per month from salary	Goal aligns with long-term aim of homeownership	December 2025
[Your Entry]	[Your Entry]	[Your Entry]	[Your Entry]	[Your Entry]	[Your Entry]

Instructions for Use:

1. **Goal Description**: Write a concise description of what you want to achieve.

2. **Specific**: Detail what you aim to accomplish with clear definitions.

3. **Measurable**: Define how you will measure the success of achieving this goal.

4. **Achievable**: Ensure the goal is realistic with the resources and time available to you.
5. **Relevant**: Confirm the goal aligns with broader personal or financial objectives.
6. **Time-bound**: Set a definitive time frame for achieving the goal.

Prioritizing Goals Worksheet

Objective: Organize and prioritize financial goals to manage resources more efficiently.

Worksheet Structure:

Goal Description	Category (Need/Want/ Wish)	Impact Level (High/Medium/ Low)	Cost Estimate	Priority
Example: Eliminate credit card debt	Need	High	$5,000	1
[Your Entry]	[Your Entry]	[Your Entry]	[Your Entry]	[Your Entry]

Instructions for Use:

1. **Goal Description**: Briefly describe each financial goal.
2. **Category**: Classify as a 'Need', 'Want', or 'Wish'.
3. **Impact Level**: Assess the impact of achieving this goal on your financial health.
4. **Cost Estimate**: Estimate how much it will cost to achieve this goal.
5. **Priority**: Rank each goal based on urgency and importance, with 1 being most critical.

Incremental Milestones Worksheet

Objective: Break down larger financial goals into manageable milestones.

Worksheet Structure:

Main Goal	Milestone	Deadline	Status	Notes
Example: Buy a house	Save $5,000 for initial home savings	Dec 2024	In Progress	Review savings strategy quarterly
[Your Entry]	[Your Entry]	[Your Entry]	[Your Entry]	[Your Entry]

Instructions for Use:

1. **Main Goal**: State the larger financial goal.
2. **Milestone**: Define smaller, actionable steps towards the main goal.
3. **Deadline**: Set a realistic deadline for each milestone.
4. **Status**: Update the current status (Not Started, In Progress, Completed).
5. **Notes**: Add any relevant notes or reminders for future review.

How to Implement

- **Regularly Update**: Ensure each worksheet is kept up-to-date with the latest information and progress. Review and adjust the worksheets at regular intervals, such as monthly or quarterly, to reflect changes in your financial situation or goals.
- **Digital or Physical Format**: Depending on your preference, maintain these worksheets either in a digital format (using a spreadsheet tool like Microsoft Excel or Google Sheets) or print them out and file them in a binder for manual updates.

- **Reflection and Adjustment**: Use these worksheets not just for tracking but also as tools for reflection. Assess what's working and what isn't, and make adjustments to your strategies accordingly to stay on track with your financial goals.

CONCLUSION

Financial literacy is not just a skill—it is a lifelong journey that empowers individuals to take control of their financial future. This eBook has aimed to provide you with a comprehensive roadmap, covering the foundational principles of budgeting, saving, mindful spending, debt management, and credit health, all the way to advanced topics like investing and building multiple income streams.

Through practical exercises, real-world examples, and actionable advice, you have been equipped with tools to navigate the complexities of personal finance confidently. Yet, the real power lies in taking action. Knowledge without application is merely potential. By implementing the lessons from each chapter, you are not just improving your financial habits—you are investing in a future defined by security, independence, and opportunity.

Key Takeaways:

1. **Budgeting is the Foundation:** Everything in personal finance ties back to budgeting. A well-structured budget ensures you live within your means, plan for emergencies, and achieve your financial goals.

2. **Mindful Spending Yields Freedom:** Aligning your spending with your values not only curbs unnecessary expenses but also brings lasting satisfaction.

3. **Debt Management is Key:** Understanding and managing debt responsibly ensures that borrowing works for you, not against you.
4. **Your Credit Score Matters:** A high credit score opens doors to better opportunities, lower interest rates, and greater financial flexibility.
5. **Investing Builds Wealth:** Starting early and harnessing the power of compound interest is crucial to growing your wealth over time.
6. **Diversify Income Streams:** Relying on a single income source is risky; multiple income streams ensure stability and accelerate financial independence.

As you move forward, remember that setbacks are part of the journey. What matters is your commitment to adapt, learn, and stay consistent. Financial success isn't about perfection—it's about progress. Whether you're just beginning to create a budget, tackling your first investment, or building new income streams, every step you take brings you closer to your goals.

This guide is more than a book—it is a resource you can revisit as your financial journey evolves. Keep refining your strategies, set new goals, and remember that financial freedom is within your reach. The power to transform your life is in your hands.

Final Note:

I hope this book has helped you shift the way you think about money and empowered you to take real steps toward financial confidence and independence.

Your financial journey is uniquely yours, and I'm honored that you let me be a part of it. If this book made a difference in your life, even in a small way, I'd be incredibly grateful if you took a moment to leave a review.

Reviews not only help others discover this book, but they also help me continue creating tools and resources that support people just like you.

You can leave a review wherever you purchased the book or share your thoughts with me at masteringmoneybook@gmail.com — I'd love to hear your story!

Thank you again for reading. Here's to your financial freedom and future abundance.

With appreciation,

Jason Broome

www.ingramcontent.com/pod-product-compliance
Lightning Source LLC
LaVergne TN
LVHW050937210926
848482LV00013B/644